Did You Know?

A collection of the most interesting facts, stories and trivia...ever!

Volume One

Written By

Cori Anne Weber,
Ramsey Mohsen,
Justin Gardner &
Larry Mitchell

Illustrations By

Damian Blake

Published by Did You Know Publishing.

ISBN-13: 978-0-9982050-0-7

Printed in the United States of America.

10 9 8 7 6 5 4 3 2 1

All illustrations © Everhance LLC.

Dedicated to our fans and all those who love to learn.

Live as if you were to die tomorrow.
Learn as if you were to live forever.

- Mahatma Gandhi

Octopuses are older than dinosaurs.

Cats get stressed out when you pet them.
Studies show cats release hormones
linked to anxiety when being pet, and the
more petting they tolerate, the more
stressed they are.

More people are killed by food each year than spiders, venomous snakes, and scorpions combined.

The older you get the happier you are. Older people tend to be happier because they're better at letting go of disappointments, but studies show that older brains also lose cognitive ability - making it easier to only concentrate on simple, happy thoughts.

Researchers studying the effects of LSD found that the drug causes separated regions of your brain to connect while also breaking down established neural networks. This mix-up of information can ease anxiety, especially in the terminally ill, because it creates an 'ego death' that causes people to lose their sense of self and feel connected to the universe.

Superman took down the KKK. The 1940s Adventures of Superman radio show revealed the Klan's secret rituals and code words in an episode series called "Clan of the Fiery Cross." Within 2 weeks, their membership had drastically declined, and people were showing up to mock them at their own rallies.

George Washington was almost 40 years old when Beethoven was born.

Thomas Edison is the reason we say 'hello' to each other. When Alexander Graham Bell invented the telephone, he wanted us to say 'ahoy' because it had been a popular greeting for over 100 years. 'Hello' was mostly used to get someone's attention (Hey, you!), but Edison thought phones would only be for businesses and therefore felt it was more appropriate.

Eating a carb and protein snack an hour before bed will help you sleep. Protein makes your brain produce melatonin and serotonin, chemicals needed for sleep, and carbs help your body absorb it.

The deep sea is 103 million square miles in area, which is larger than all of the land on Earth.

The Big Bang theory was invented by a Catholic priest. Monseigneur Georges Lemaître proposed that the beginning of the universe was a "Cosmic Egg exploding at the moment of the creation," which later became known as the Big Bang.

AOL still makes millions of dollars from dial-up subscribers.

The Huns had no writing system. They were completely illiterate, so every record of them was written by their enemies - who all describe them as hideous savages.

Suburban American households put out so many Christmas lights, they can be seen from space. NASA combined satellite images of U.S. cities (those that weren't covered in snow) and found that America glows brighter the day after Thanksgiving and doesn't quit until New Year's Day.

The place where Julius Caesar was murdered later became a cat sanctuary. One of Rome's many stray cat shelters sits next to the site of the Theatre of Pompey, and some say the cats of Rome are older than the Roman civilization itself.

In 2014, the rare Kashmir musk deer was spotted in its historic Afghani range for the first time in 66 years. These endangered deer have long fangs and are killed for their scent glands, which are used in perfumes and are more valuable than gold.

Looking at your own Facebook profile temporarily boosts your self-esteem.

Veronika Scott turned a college assignment into a nonprofit company that's helping the homeless. She's hired many women from Detroit's homeless shelters, and together they've made thousands of sleeping bag coats to give to people who are living on the streets.

On April 11, 1954...nothing happened. No major events were recorded. It was the most boring day in history - until people noticed. Then it became interesting for being so incredibly boring.

Ed Damiano developed a bionic pancreas for his son, who needed constant management of his insulin pump. It worked so well, the people using it for a trial were sad to give it back.

Abraham Lincoln dreamed about being assassinated 3 nights in a row before he was shot. Crook, his bodyguard, told him to stay home that night, but he left anyway and said "Goodbye, Crook." It was the first time he'd ever told him goodbye instead of 'good night.'

In America, blonde women are generally paid more for the same job than women with other hair colors.

France has more time zones than Russia or the United States.

The Krusty Krab restaurant on SpongeBob SquarePants is modeled after a New England lobster-trap. The traps are the same shape and have a "kitchen" and "parlor." The Krusty Krab has a kitchen and a dining area, as well as a "lockdown mode," suggesting that it may have been made out of a real lobster-trap.

The Roman Colosseum used to have a retractable roof. The 'velarium' was a sloped canvas awning that covered 2/3 of the arena and acted as a ventilation system to catch the wind and create a breeze for the spectators.

The oldest living tree ever found was a pine named "Prometheus." It had been alive since before the Egyptian pyramids were built. Some guy cut it down in 1964.

Jealous men try to have more sex. A study found that a man who thinks his female partner is exceptionally attractive tries to have sex with her more often if she has a lot of male friends and co-workers.

Flying with your pets isn't always safe. Each year dozens of pets are killed, injured, and lost because airlines treat pets as cargo. In these instances, corrective action is almost never taken.

As part of a charity stunt to protest Black Friday, Cards Against Humanity got 30,000 people to buy actual bullshit in a box. They made it clear that they were selling "literal feces, from a literal bull," but still sold out. Their cow poop profits were donated to help end hunger and poverty.

It's been estimated that there are more stars in the Universe than there are grains of sand on earth, but there are more atoms in one grain of sand than there are stars in the Universe.

Lucy and Maria Aylmer are twins, but they have a hard time convincing people. Even though they have mixed-race parents, their mom was still shocked when the midwife handed her babies she'd expected to look alike, but were complete opposites.

Your body is shrinking, and it's never going to stop. Once you reach your 30s, you lose 1/2 an inch in height every 10 years.

Your reaction to maggots can reveal if you're a liberal or a conservative. The brain scans of liberals looking at photos of maggots and carcasses are so different from conservatives' that scientists can review them and predict the person's political preference with 95% accuracy.

Einstein's career was greatly influenced by his partying. As a young man he was part of a drinking club where friends got drunk and debated philosophy and science, and where he and his wife were once "alas, dead drunk under the table." He later said that the club had a big effect on his career.

Every planet in the solar system can fit between the Earth and the Moon, but the Sun can't. Even 1/3 of the Sun would be too big to fit.

The first radio communication from an
aircraft in flight was: "Roy, come and
get this goddamn cat!"

Frano Selak escaped certain death 7
times, then bought his very first lotto
ticket and won nearly a million dollars. He
then decided to give away his entire
fortune because money can't buy
happiness, and all he needs is his wife.

Your brain can make you irrational if you have cognitive dissonance, which is two conflicting beliefs that make you uncomfortable. This is why a smoker might refuse to believe that smoking causes lung cancer - the brain tries to eliminate the cause of dissonance, and quitting is more difficult than not believing something.

When Koko the gorilla met Robin Williams in 2001, he made her smile for the first time in over 6 months. After Williams died in 2014, Koko overheard the news and signed the word "cry."

Caffeine withdrawal is officially a mental disorder, according to the American Psychiatric Association.

Annette Kellerman was one of the first to design a one-piece suit for swimming instead of a dress and pantaloons. In 1907, she wore her suit to the beach. She was arrested for indecency.

Video games give you better morals. Studies show that doing bad stuff in virtual worlds can make you feel guilty, which makes you nicer in real life.

The groove in the middle of your top lip is there for a reason. It is called a "philtrum," and it's where 3 sections of your face fused together when you developed in the womb.

Sad music makes you happier. Listening to sad music when you're upset helps your mood because it feels like someone is consoling you. Happy music can make you feel worse, like a perky person telling you to smile when you're pissed.

One of the most popular Christmas toys in 1975 was a rock in a box. Gary Dahl's novelty invention, "Pet Rock," was a smooth stone that came in a cardboard box with instructions for "care and feeding." The fad only lasted for about 6 months, but Dahl made $2 million.

N'kisi, an African grey parrot with a 950 word vocabulary, impressed the famous primatologist Jane Goodall. N'kisi had seen photos of her, and when they met he asked, "Got a chimp?"

The plural of octopus is not 'octopi.' Technically it should be 'octopodes,' but 'octopuses' is standard for the English language.

Alexis Goggins was only 7 when she and her mom were held at gunpoint inside a car. Alexis jumped in front of her mother and took 6 bullets to save her. Doctors said she'd never walk or talk again. She not only walked, she told them she wasn't a hero, she was just saving her mom.

In 1938, a forest warden in what used to be Communist East Germany planted trees in the shape of a swastika that could only be seen when leaves turned in the fall. It wasn't rediscovered until 1992.

In 18th century London, the price of admission to an exotic animal zoo was 3 half-pence, but if you were short on cash you could bring a cat or dog as payment. They fed them to the lions.

Just like humans, dogs have a left and right brain. Researchers found that dogs also process speech in the same pattern as humans: language on the left side of their brain, and emotions on the right.

A study found female scientists are consistently judged as less competent and offered lower salaries than males with identical qualifications - even if they were being hired by other female scientists.

If you're looking for a job, your application and resume style aren't nearly as important as having an inside referral. Knowing someone who works at the company increases your chance of getting an interview and makes you 40% more likely to get the job over someone with a fancier resume.

Jock McLaren cheated death many times, then died accidentally. He fought in both WWI and WWII, battled guerrillas in Singapore, escaped from prison camps, and removed his own appendix with a mirror and a pocket knife while being chased by the Japanese. He was finally killed when rotted wood fell on him after he backed a car into a tree.

About 80% of all blindness can be avoided, prevented, or cured.

You feel healthier and happier from Friday night to Sunday afternoon. People from all pay grades report more ailments during the work week. This "weekend effect" shows that having free time is essential to your well-being.

Broken Heart Syndrome is a real medical condition brought on by tragedy or shock, and it feels like a heart attack. A surge of stress hormones causes a temporary disruption in your heart's normal pumping function, giving you chest pain and shortness of breath.

The 7th President of the United States was a murderer. On May 30, 1806, Andrew Jackson cheated during a duel to kill his rival, a man who publicly attacked him and his wife by publishing insults about them in a newspaper.

MIT engineers created a wearable vest that hooks to an e-book and can change the lighting, sound, temperature, chest tightness, and heart rate of the reader so they can experience what the character in the book is feeling.

Part of Amelia Earhart's lost plane may have been discovered on the island of Nikumaroro. A piece of aluminum found in 1991 was of no interest to researchers until 2014, when they noticed a shiny patch in a photo near the tail of the plane that could be a match.

Tigers are very sneaky hunters. They will imitate the calls of other animals so they can attract them as prey.

Male kangaroos flex their biceps to impress females. Kangaroo males need strength to fight off their rivals, and researchers found they deliberately show off their muscles in order to attract a mate.

When you receive a kidney transplant, your own kidney isn't removed. It usually stays where it is and a third kidney is placed in your pelvis.

The United States endures about 75% of the world's known tornadoes. Most of them happen in Texas, which gets an annual average of 166 tornadoes spread out over every month of the year.

Ancient Egyptians knew more about medicine than people from the Middle Ages. In 1550 BC, Egyptians had a decent understanding of the circulatory system. But in 1553 AD, Miguel Serveto realized that blood circulated through the lungs and was burned at the stake for heresy.

Captain Hook was based on a real man with similar problems. John Maher was an ex-pirate who posed as a pastor to hide from an enemy. When he was found his enemy stalked him until he went insane, just like Hook and the tick-tock croc.

After puppies are born, they see their mom eating their feces to keep them clean, and they pick up the habit as well. Some of them outgrow it, but others get addicted and can't quit. That's why dogs eat poop.

Trick candles keep burning for the same reason that road flares and sparklers do: magnesium. When you blow out a regular candle, an ember glows in the wick, but the vaporized wax keeps it from lighting again. Since trick candle wicks have magnesium in them, the wick ember reignites every time.

The only breed of dog to be mentioned by name in the Bible is the greyhound.

Dr. Seuss's first book was rejected 27 times. He was ready to give up when he bumped into a friend on the street who'd just begun working in publishing. Seuss said if he'd been walking on the other side of the street, he probably would never have been a children's author.

U.S. states that use the death penalty have consistently higher murder rates than non-death-penalty states.

If you want to improve your golf swing, you need more sleep. During REM sleep your brain converts short-term motor memories into long-term muscle memories. A good night's sleep is essential to improving your athletic performance.

The first line of code ever written by a U.S. president was moveForward(100);. Barack Obama sat with students who were learning JavaScript through a tutorial game based on the movie Frozen. The President's code was a function that moved Elsa's character forward 100-pixels.

Death row inmates in America are more likely to die of old age than execution.

80% of the world's seafloor was unmapped until 2014, when satellites explored the Atlantic and revealed ancient underwater rifts. Scientists think this technology will help us understand greater depths and find more mineral resources.

People were "unfriending" each other long before Facebook. In 1659, an English clergyman wrote, "I hope, sir, that we are not mutually un-friended by this difference which hath happened betwixt us."

When you start to panic, because you're about to introduce someone and you can't remember their name, don't feel too bad. It's such a frequent occurrence that the Scots have their own word for it: tartle.

Whether you're naughty or nice depends on your name. A website that tracks the behavior of school children made a list of the best and worst of 2014. Jacob, Daniel, Thomas, Amy, Emma, and Grace were the names of the nicest children; and Joseph, Jake, Cameron, Ella, Bethany, and Laura were all pretty naughty.

When George Lucas sold his company to Disney, he vowed to donate most of his $4 billion Star Wars wealth to education. He launched his foundation to improve grades K-12 because he believes education is the key to the survival of the human race.

Lightning strikes 100 times per second worldwide. That's enough electricity to light 8.6 million light bulbs for 3 months.

Baby elephants suck on their trunks for comfort, just like human babies suck their thumbs. Adult elephants do it too. Trunk-sucking is most common in the young, but even old bulls suck their trunks when they feel nervous or unsure.

Middle-aged bees become undertakers. Some older bees have the job of removing all the dead bee bodies from the hive. They pick them up, carry them 300 feet away, then drop them.

Your dog can hear your sadness. Researchers recently discovered that dogs have a specific section of their brain that only exists to process the human voice and its emotion. Humans also have a specific section of brain that only processes dog vocalizations.

Doctors' unsanitized stethoscopes transmit more germs than their hands. A recent study showed that stethoscopes are very germy, because while most doctors wash their hands regularly, many of them forget to clean their stethoscopes.

Going to an elite college might not be worth it. Most students attending prestigious schools end up with greater debt and with earnings no higher than students who didn't choose the best school they could get into.

People who understand sarcasm are good mind readers. Because sarcasm is a sort of "true lie," you have to find the real meaning behind words that aren't meant literally, differentiating between someone's false emotions and what they're really thinking. If you can easily detect a well-hidden sarcastic comment, you likely have great social intuition.

The oldest art of all time was found on a 540,000-year-old shell. Researchers in Indonesia discovered ancient carvings on a seashell that indicate Homo erectus may have been smarter than we thought.

It's illegal to abandon your parents in China. Anyone whose parents are older than 60 is legally required to visit them often and make sure their financial and spiritual needs are being met.

Young female chimps use sticks as dolls and care for them as babies. The discovery of this behavior is the 1st example of wild animals of both sexes playing with objects in different ways, which suggests that the preference of feminine or masculine toys is biological and not learned.

Andrew Jackson's pet parrot was removed from his funeral for cussing incessantly.

Women can see more shades of red than men. The gene that allows us to see the color red is on the X chromosome, of which men only have 1. Because women have 2, they can see crimson, maroon, cardinal, ruby, and scarlet, but men may only see light red and dark red.

We figured out how to travel to the moon before we learned to put wheels on our suitcases.

The foreskins of circumcised babies are often used as skin graft tissue, to help manufacture human skin, and to make anti-wrinkle skin creams.

The farther a cat falls, the better. Cats are less likely to be injured if they fall from greater heights. When cats fall from 5 stories or higher, they reach terminal velocity and relax their bodies, which slows them down and protects them from the impact.

Spirit animals are a representation of you or what you want to become. They were originally a concept of Native American spirituality, but a driving force that helped them go viral was Tumblr users. Honorable mention goes to Samuel L. Jackson.

Your heart is so powerful that it can squirt blood 30 feet across the room.

There's a salt flat in Bolivia that turns into an endless mirror when it rains. Salar de Uyuni is the world's largest salt flat, formed from prehistoric lakes that dried out and left behind a flat crust of salt that spans 4,086 square miles.

Sea World has ended their orca captive breeding program. They also plan to move from performing with the orcas to providing more natural encounters. The current orca generation will be the last in captivity for Sea World.

Snow is white because snowflakes are complex. Their intricate, complicated structures don't allow light to pass through. All the wavelengths of light are reflected, which makes the snow appear white.

70% of managers are making their teams worse. Gallup scientists found that companies are hiring the wrong people to be managers or supervisors 82% of the time, wasting time and money and causing their employees to become disengaged.

Illegal immigrants in the U.S. provide about $15 billion a year to Social Security. Without their contributions, the Social Security Administration would have been paying out more money than it received since the year 2009.

Before he passed away in 2009, Kim Peek could memorize an entire book in an hour. He read 2 pages at a time, scanning one with each eye. He remembered the contents of 12,000 books and was the inspiration for Dustin Hoffman's character in the film Rain Man. When they met, Hoffman said "I may be the star, but you are the heavens."

Night vision goggles show green because the human eye can see more shades of green than any other color.

The U.S. had 3 different presidents in the year 1881. Hayes finished his term, and then Garfield was elected, but he only served 4 months before he was assassinated and Chester Arthur took over. A similar situation also happened in 1841 with Van Buren, Harrison, and Tyler.

Rap battles have been around since the 5th century. 'Flyting' was a ritual in which two people competed by exchanging insults in poetic verse, similar to modern freestyle battles between rappers. The insults were very provocative, and people often accused each other of cowardice and sexual perversion.

It is an old Japanese tradition that the first dream of a new year will come true.

A blue-skinned family lived in Kentucky in the 1800s. "The Blue Fugates" had a condition called methemoglobinemia that limits oxygen in the body's tissues. Because of the family's inbreeding, many of them had blue skin.

There is a website that lets you download YouTube videos to your computer. You just insert the word 'Magic' between the two words "you" and "tube" in the URL of the video you want to download.

The Spanish Ribbed Newt is like an amphibian version of Wolverine. It uses its spiky ribs as a defense mechanism by pushing them through its own skin to release venom, and then it quickly heals itself.

Pigeons can recognize videos of themselves that have a 7-second delay, which is something 3-year-old humans can't do. They can't even recognize themselves in a video that has a 2-second-delay.

Reading Harry Potter makes kids more accepting of others. Psychologists found that reading the Potter series improved young people's tolerance of immigrants, homosexuals, and other stigmatized groups.

The sun isn't yellow, it's white. We see it as a particular color because of the light that's able to pass through the atmosphere. Most photos of the sun have been altered to be the color that we are used to seeing, but in space it's just white.

Salvador Dali didn't always pay at restaurants. He was known for drawing sketches on the back of his checks because he knew that the restaurant wouldn't want to cash a valuable piece of art.

The traditional New Year's song, "Auld Lang Syne," means "days gone by." About 3/4 of people admit they make up the words, because they have no idea what the lyrics are.

People who grew up without color television have different dreams. In the 1940s, 75% of Americans claimed they "rarely" or "never" dreamed in color. But recent studies show that now only 12% report dreaming in black-and-white.

Norwegian police don't use guns. In Norway, only 2 people have been shot and killed by police in the past decade. When the officers are faced with danger, they back out, form a plan, and try to solve the problem without using firearms.

If someone says you're blind as a bat, they're complimenting your vision. Bats can see extremely well. They use echolocation to find the distance between themselves and their prey, not to "see" them.

If you slip on the ice and hit your head this winter, you don't have to stay awake all night if you have a concussion. Falling asleep won't hurt you (your body actually needs the rest), but you may need to be woken up every 2 hours to make sure you haven't developed new symptoms.

Mike Anderson was sentenced to 13 years in prison. When his order to report to jail never came, he turned his life around, started a family, and opened his own business. The jail discovered the error on his 'release date' 13 years later and imprisoned him for 10 months, but a judge let him go because he was a 'changed man' and jail no longer served a purpose.

Turquoise Elfcup, Hairy Parachute, Cinnamon Jellybaby, Weeping Toothcrust, Witches' Butter, and Hairy Nuts Disco are all types of mushrooms.

The Rubik's Cube was invented because Erno Rubik wanted to build a structure with pieces that move independently without falling apart. He had no idea he was creating the best-selling toy of all time until he scrambled it and tried to fix it. It took him a month to figure it out.

If you die alone at home, your pets will eat you. Dogs might wait several days until they're starved for food, but cats will likely eat you within a day or two.

In Japan, it is a common belief that blood type determines your personality, much like the zodiac. Food and hygiene products are made for different blood types, and magazines publish blood type horoscopes.

A dog's nose print is just like a human fingerprint. The nose print of a dog is so unique that nose printing has been proposed as a more effective way to identify your pet than micro-chipping.

In 1967, Australian Prime Minister Harold Holt went swimming at Cheviot Beach and completely vanished. People went crazy and blamed UFOs and Chinese submarines for his disappearance. His body was never found.

In the 19th century Holland, a Protestant man and his Catholic wife weren't allowed to be buried in the same lot, so they turned their graves into a monument that holds hands over the wall that divides them.

Chewing gum before your next test could raise your grade. Studies showed students who chewed gum for 5 minutes before testing had better scores. The chewing motion increases blood flow to your brain and boosts your memory, but chewing too long takes too much brainpower and makes you tired.

In Sierra Leone, citizens have to play a board game to get a driver's license. The game is called The Drivers' Way, costs wannabe drivers about $14, and they have to play it at least once before they can even take the test.

Brother huskies Gonzo and Poncho were on a dog sled team, but Gonzo went blind. He wanted to keep running, so Poncho began to nudge him in the right direction. Now Gonzo leans on his brother so they can run together every day.

Over a 1/4 of Americans pray for their sports teams. According to a 2014 study, almost half of surveyed Americans believe God determines the winner, especially if it's a football game.

You can visit your dog when you're not at home. PetChatz is a video monitor that lets you spy on your dog, say hello, give out treats, and dispense calming smells by using your phone or PC to control the system from anywhere.

90% of the world's population uses caffeine, even though 100 mg a day (about 1 cup of coffee) can cause dependence.

NASA emailed a wrench to space. An astronaut working on the International Space Station needed a tool he didn't have, so NASA designed one with computer software and emailed the file to him. He then used a 3D printer to create the first object ever designed on Earth and made in space.

Dan Aykroyd used to call John Belushi 'America's Guest.' When Belushi went missing from The Blues Brothers set at 3am one night, Aykroyd asked a nearby homeowner if he'd seen one of their actors. He replied: 'Oh, you mean Belushi? He came in here an hour ago and raided my fridge. He's asleep on the couch.'

The ROYGBIV acronym is a big understatement. There are more colors in the rainbow than there are stars in the universe or atoms in your body, but even a perfect human eye could only see about a million of them.

On the morning of Pakistan's Peshawar school massacre, 15-year-old Dawood Ibrahim saved his own life by sleeping through his alarm. Every student from his class was killed. His older brother believes it was fate, because Dawood is alive, but class 9 no longer exists.

When male and female anglerfish mate,
they melt into each other and share
bodies forever. The deep sea is so vast
that, if a male finds a female, he latches on
and fuses to her, losing his eyes and
internal organs until the two fish
share a bloodstream.

Putting on a red shirt makes women find
you more attractive. Many studies have
shown that women are culturally and
biologically attracted to men wearing red.

A design student in Vienna created a water bottle for your bike that attaches to the frame and collects moisture from the air, which turns into water as you ride. On a humid day, it can produce 0.5 liters of water in an hour.

In 1961, an 8-year-old girl wrote a letter to President Kennedy because she was worried about Santa being hurt by the Soviets testing nuclear bombs. He wrote her back to tell her not to worry, because he'd talked to Santa, and he was OK.

The 2014 winter solstice was not the "longest night ever." While the Earth's rotation is slowing due to tidal friction, it has also sped up over the last 40 years in response to the redistributed mass from the loss of polar ice sheets. So the "longest night ever" was actually in 1912.

While there are about 14 correct spellings of the Jewish holiday, 'Chanukah,' often used by traditionalists, was the most popular spelling on the Internet 5 years ago. Today, 'Hanukkah' has become mainstream because English speakers better understand how to pronounce it when it begins with an H.

Gambling generates more revenue than recorded music, movies, cruise ships, theme parks, and spectator sports combined. It's a $40 billion a year industry in the U.S. alone.

You don't have the stomach flu. There's actually no such thing. If you're violently oozing out of both ends, you have gastroenteritis caused by a virus, bacteria, or food poisoning.

Australia's Gippsland Lakes can glow in the dark. Flooding and a growing number of micro-organisms in the summer of 2009 caused the often bioluminescent lake to be brighter than ever. Even the people who swam in it were glowing blue.

Graham crackers and Kellogg's corn flakes were invented to stop people from masturbating. Their inventors both believed that eating bland foods would suppress sexual desires and unhealthy urges.

NASA intoxicated spiders with different drugs to see if they could still build an effective web. All of the drugs reduced web regularity except for small doses of LSD, which actually increased it.

There are sharks that can survive in fresh water. Scientists once thought the freshwater sharks in Lake Nicaragua were their own species, but it turned out they were just bull sharks that adapted to living in fresh water by urinating 20 times more than saltwater sharks.

When filming Home Alone, Macaulay Culkin was friends with Michael Jackson and slept in his bedroom. He testified at Jackson's trial that the sexual allegations were "ridiculous," that the bedroom was two stories tall, and that he was never touched inappropriately.

You burn fat when you breathe. When the body breaks down fat compounds during exercise, a portion of it turns into carbon dioxide and leaves your body through your lungs each time you exhale.

Men crave steak and women want chocolate because of American advertising. There are no biological reasons for either food to be gender specific. Studies have shown that women in outside countries don't report having chocolate cravings (even during PMS), and that men like steak or chocolate just as much as their female counterparts.

Every year, an estimated 4.68 million trees are used to make phone books. Nearly 2/3 of them end up in landfills.

Ravens can imitate human speech. Their voices are deep and similar to a man's, and some can learn to talk better than parrots. They're also able to mimic wolf and fox calls to lead them to a carcass they want to eat but can't open.

If we had faster spacecrafts, we could travel into the future. At incredibly high speeds, time dilation would allow humans to travel the entire known universe in one lifetime and return to Earth billions of years in the future.

You can win an argument by using 'extreme agreement.' For example: instead of asking a political radical 'why' they want a specific change, asking them 'how' they suggest making that change will soften their views, because you've turned the idea into something too extreme to accomplish.

Taste is highly influenced by color. Hot chocolate tastes better when served in an orange or cream-colored cup than in a red one, according to studies. The color of a coffee cup also affects people's perception of how strong the brew is.

Male dragonflies compete to become dads. They have a spoonlike penis that they use to scoop out the sperm of rival males before depositing their own inside a female.

Women can have a much longer orgasm than men. The average male orgasm lasts up to 10 seconds, but a female's can last longer than 20 seconds.

Saying 'thank you' makes you happier. Researchers found that people who express gratitude are usually more content, couples who are openly grateful for their partner are more comfortable in their relationships, and employees who are thanked by their managers often work up to 50% harder.

Music affects the way you perceive reality. Listening to particularly happy music can make you see smiling faces where there are none. The same holds true for sad music, which causes you to perceive exaggerated sadness.

Victor Lustig was such a good con artist, he sold the Eiffel Tower. He convinced scrap-metal dealers that the tower was too expensive for the city to maintain, and sold it for $70,000. He later sold it again, but the buyer reported him to the police. He's now famously known as "The man who sold the Eiffel Tower. Twice."

The rapper known as Nelly has paid the full college tuition of 2 kids in need of financial assistance every year since 2005.

Belly button lint is blue because most people often wear blue or gray pants. It's a ball of dead skin, fat, sweat, dust, and cotton fibers that are pulled off your clothes by navel hairs, which have tiny barbs that hook onto fabrics and funnel in small bits of fluff. The larger and hairier you are, the more lint you make.

Rudolph was almost "Rollo the Not-Red-Nosed Reindeer." When Robert L. May created Rudolph in 1939, he considered using the name Rollo, and the story was originally rejected because a red nose was associated with being a drunk.

Most of the world's oxygen comes from the ocean. About 70% of Earth's oxygen is produced by phytoplankton, which also remove most of the carbon dioxide from the atmosphere.

A Jewish father who wanted to start a fun, new tradition with his sons created "Mensch on a Bench." In the spirit of "Elf on the Shelf," Moshe the Mensch comes with a book that teaches kids about Hanukkah.

Over 40% of Americans make New Year's resolutions, but only 8% achieve them. Deciding to 'lose some weight' sets you up for failure, but saying 'I'm going to stop eating french fries for 2 months' is attainable. Approaching your goal in smaller steps is a more successful strategy.

Researchers are developing a graphene contact lens that lets the wearer see UV and infrared light. The lenses would let soldiers in combat zones spot heat signatures and doctors monitor blood flow in their patients' bodies.

Approximately 1 million marine species live in our oceans, but researchers estimate that over 600,000 of them haven't been formally described or named.

Evidence of the oldest man/dog relationship is in a French cave. Side-by-side foot and paw prints were discovered in the mud of Chauvet Cave in 1994. The 26,000-year-old tracks were left by a barefoot boy of 8 and his wolf companion, and they were completely untouched when they were discovered.

You're always living in the past. Everything you see is on a slight delay, so what you're looking at right now is an average of what you've seen in the past 10-15 seconds. Your brain filters out unimportant information, so you don't go crazy with all the stimuli in your environment.

In 1960, Dr. Frances Oldham Kelsey stood against corporate pressure and refused to approve the USA's release of thalidomide, a tranquilizer prescribed to pregnant women. During her first month working for the FDA, she saved countless lives because the drug was found to cause serious birth defects.

The average person falls in love twice. Men and women both report falling "head-over-heels" only twice in their lifetime, and 1 out of 7 feel they are settling for their current partner because true love "slipped through their fingers."

The 'fairy tale' image of medieval princesses is completely warped. Taking history into account, if you say you want to be "treated like a princess," you're really saying that you want to live in a filthy castle; smell like death, sewage and B.O.; and be married off as a teenager to an old foreign guy.

In 2011, engineers building a dam in the Amazon discovered an Atretochoana eiselti, a creature that has earned many nicknames, including penis snake. It breathes through its skin, can't see much, and is an amphibian even though it looks like a snake (among other things).

The scent of Thanksgiving can give men a boner. Smelling lavender and pumpkin pie each increased blood flow to the penis by 40%, according to research.

There's a 'Normal Barbie' doll that has brown hair and the measurements of an average 19-year-old girl. It comes with stickers that give the doll acne, cellulite, stretch marks, scars, freckles, and moles in hopes to teach kids that real life is cool.

If you crack an egg in the ocean, it will remain intact. Divers went 60 ft underwater and found there's enough pressure to hold the yolk and white of a cracked egg together as if it were still in its shell.

Sex makes you smarter. Having sex improves cognitive function and increases the rate of new brain cells being formed, giving you more brainpower. But it doesn't work in reverse, because smarter people usually have less sex.

Edgar Allen Poe predicted the future. His only novel is about 4 shipwrecked men who run out of food and eat the cabin boy, Richard Parker. 46 years after it published, a yacht sank in real life, and 3 of the 4 survivors also decided to eat the cabin boy...named Richard Parker.

Bicultural people may change their personalities when they switch languages. According to a study, language unconsciously affects people's interpretation of events. Women speaking Spanish were seen as more independent and assertive than women speaking English in similar situations.

If your parents referred to sex as the "birds and the bees," they were very wrong. Nearly all male birds don't even have a penis, and after drone bees mate with the queen, their penis explodes and they die.

Dogs like to align themselves with the North-South axis when they poop. They do this whenever the Earth's magnetic field conditions are normal - but if they're unstable, dogs get confused and turn around in circles before doing their business.

There could be a permanent village on the moon by 2036. The European Space Agency plans to start building a lunar community in the next 20 years to establish a base for scientific research, though it could also be used for mining or tourism.

This baby elephant took down 14 lions. After straying from his mom, lions attacked the 1-year-old elephant. He outsmarted them when, recognizing their hatred of water, he ran into a watering hole to fight them off. He was later reunited with his family and given the name Hercules because of his courage and strength.

Apple has a patent for a system that can protect your iPhone if you drop it. The system can re-orient your phone during a fall and change the angle of impact to prevent as much damage as possible.

You're more likely to donate to 1 person than to millions, because the good feeling you get from helping clashes with the bad feeling that you can't help that many people. So you won't do what you can do, because you feel bad about what you can't do.

Bad bosses are expensive. They cost the American economy $360 billion each year. They also cause chronic stress, contagious depression, illness, strokes, and heart attacks, according to various studies.

Having trouble skipping stones? Scientists found that tilting them at a 20-degree angle in your hand and also throwing them toward the water at a 20-degree angle is the key to making them bounce as many times as possible.

A pit bull named Tiger saved his owner's life. When Todd Kibbey passed out on the front porch, Tiger ran to a neighbor's house and cried until she noticed him. If she hadn't walked him home and found Todd unconscious, he would have died.

10-year-old Willie Myrick was saved by the gospel. After being abducted from his front yard, he sang the song "Every Praise" for 3 hours straight until his kidnapper finally kicked him out of the car. He later met gospel singer Hezekiah Walker, and they sang the song as a duet.

Your appendix could actually be useful. There's evidence that it functions as a 'safe house' for good bacteria, which can flush out infection in your large intestine.

All snowflakes are different because of how they travel to the ground. As they fall, atmospheric changes cause different patterns of ice crystals to form. Because each one has a different journey, no two are alike.

Your cell phone could save your life. A Brazilian police officer had his Nokia Lumia 520 in his back pocket when two criminals began shooting at him. He was shot in the butt as he ran away, but the phone took the bullet, and he was unharmed.

Poinsettias are not poisonous. They can irritate your eyes and skin, cause an upset stomach, and their fibrous leaves are easy for cats and kids to choke on, but unless you're allergic, eating them won't kill you.

The 3 inmates who escaped from Alcatraz may have survived. A recent study suggests that if they left at midnight they could have made it to land, but if they left even an hour earlier or later, the tide would have worked against them, and they would have died of hypothermia.

Beethoven's 9th Symphony is performed throughout Japan during the New Years season. The song was introduced to the Japanese by German prisoners of war who were held in Japan during WWI. It became so popular, it's now an annual holiday tradition.

The National Day of Mourning and Unthanksgiving Day are U.S. events held in protest of Thanksgiving. Participants consider the holiday a reminder of the democide of Native Americans and want to educate people about their true history.

Tampons, cigarette butts, and Silly String are all used by soldiers in battle. Tampons plug bullet wounds, cigarette butts keep gun barrels clear, and Silly String can make trip-wires visible without setting them off.

Your phone can hurt you. "Text neck" happens when you lean over your phone to read or text, putting up to 60 pounds of pressure on your spine. Instead of bending your neck, looking at your phone with your head up can save you from future pain.

There is a single tree that produces 40 different types of fruit. Professor Sam Van Aken from Syracuse University spent 9 years cultivating the 'Tree of 40 Fruit,' which grows varieties of cherries, plums, peaches, nectarines, and apricots.

Children worldwide were twice as likely to die before their 5th birthday in 1990 than they are today. Since then, all regions except Sub-Saharan Africa and Oceania have reduced the under-5 death rate by 52% or more.

The wounded ozone layer above Antarctica is showing signs of healing. Balloon and satellite observations recently detected the first clear evidence that efforts to eradicate chlorofluorocarbons, which began in 1987, have had a positive, reversing effect on the ozone depletion.

Lexington, Kentucky's 'Food for Fines' program lets you pay off parking tickets with canned goods. You get a $15 credit for every 10 donated cans, which in turn supplies the program with thousands of cans for local food banks each year.

Blood donors in Sweden get a text message whenever their blood is used to save a life. The program hopes to recruit and retain more donors by highlighting their importance and getting them excited about making a difference.

Turkey doesn't have enough tryptophan to make you drowsy. If it did, you'd be tired after eating a turkey sandwich any day of the year. Eggs, cheese, spinach, and bacon all contain more tryptophan per serving than turkey - which has the same amount as chicken.

If you were sucked into space out of an airlock, your eyes wouldn't pop out, and your body wouldn't explode like in the movies. You would likely pass out after about 15 seconds and then suffocate.

Snails shoot darts that are like Cupid's arrows. About 1/3 of all snail species shoot "love darts" at each other before mating. The snails each stab their mate with a dart covered in a mucus that makes their sperm more effective and temporarily prevents mating with another snail.

Benjamin Franklin wrote a scientific essay about farts. Because he thought European academic societies were pretentious, he responded to a call for scientific papers with his essay, "Fart Proudly," which suggested research be done to improve the odor of human flatulence.

Ladies, if you have blue or green eyes, you're probably better at studying, tolerating pain, and drinking alcohol. Brown-eyed girls: you might get drunk more easily, but you're also likely to think faster and be better at sports.

The smell of women's tears turns men off. Researchers found that smelling female tears did not generate empathy from men, but instead caused their sexual arousal and testosterone levels to decrease.

The slinky was invented by accident. In 1943, engineer Richard James was trying to make a meter to monitor naval ships, when he dropped a tension spring that kept moving across the floor - giving him a great idea for a toy.

Scientists around the world explored which activities can cause an epiphany. They found that gaining a flash of insight is often triggered by activities that require little thought, such as walking, showering, or gardening, because they give your mind time to wander to another place.

Half of the Great Barrier Reef is either dead or dying, and 93% of it is now bleached. Coral bleaches when it's highly stressed due to pollution, overheating, or disease. If climate conditions do not change, most of the reef will probably disappear.

There's a 300-page book called 'A Void' that was written without ever using the letter 'e.' The original is French, but there are over a dozen versions in different languages written by translators who also managed to compose them without using the most common letter of the alphabet.

Camels' humps do not store water. They are mounds of fat that allow them to travel through the desert for days without having to eat. If they use up their supply, the hump shrinks and falls to one side until they've rested and refueled.

In 1984, all Koko the gorilla wanted for Christmas was her own pet cat. When she was given a toy cat instead, she refused to play with it and signed the word "sad" until they finally gave her a real one.

If you drink more, you earn more. Studies show drinkers earn 10-14% more money than teetotalers, and men who visit bars at least once a month earn an additional 7% more. CEOs claim it's due to the connection between socializing and career advancement.

Couples who smoke weed together are less likely to hurt each other. Studies of couples during the first 9 years of marriage found that those who frequently smoked marijuana together were less likely to engage in domestic violence.

The Winter Solstice, one of the oldest winter celebrations in the world, is important in some cultures because it marks the annual re-birth of the sun. Each year crowds gather at Stonehenge, which is aligned so that you can view the solstice sunrise from the center of the monument.

99% of teachers spend $500-$1,000 of their own money each year on class materials. Charities like Adoptaclassroom.org and Donorschoose.org let you donate to classrooms, and teachers update you with pictures to show how your money was used.

People used to be terrified of tomatoes. In the 1700s, eating tomatoes caused many deaths, but it was actually the high lead content in their pewter plates that killed them. The tomatoes just soaked up more lead because of their acidity.

Sony's VAIO logo contains a hidden message. The letters 'VA' are a sine wave, and the letters 'IO' are a 1 and 0 that symbolize the digital signals in binary code. Together, they represent technology evolving from analog to digital.

Dogs aren't just sniffing each other's butts for fun, they're communicating. The smells from another dog's anal glands can reveal their diet, gender, emotional state, and more.

89

Cavemen didn't live in caves.
Archaeologists believe they spent more
time living outside of caves than in, and
some didn't even have "homes" because
they traveled to find food.

Ancient Egyptian paint could give us
better phones. The world's 1st synthetic
pigment was "Egyptian blue," and
scientists found that it's made of
nanomaterials that can be used to
improve TV remotes, phones, satellites,
medical imaging, and the Internet.

Racism is bad for your health. People who have negative feelings toward other races, and people who experience discrimination both release more stress hormones that damage the body. Researchers found that victims of racism have higher blood pressure and a greater decline in kidney function - symptoms that are both linked to stress.

We use the terms "white meat" and "dark meat" because the Victorians were prudes. In the early 1800s, people found it vulgar to say leg, thigh, or breast - especially around women.

Play-Doh was originally used to clean wallpaper. In the 1930s, people burned coal to heat their homes and rolled the dough across the walls to lift up the soot. The product became obsolete when vinyl wallpaper and new heating methods evolved, so they sold it as a toy.

In simulation, people are much quicker to shoot black men. Researchers created an online game where the player is a cop with the goal of "shooting" pictures of men holding a gun. Players of all races routinely shot black men more quickly and were more likely to shoot an unarmed black man on accident.

If you've been leaving carrots out for Santa's reindeer, you might want to try eggs or fresh meat instead. Reindeer often eat lemmings after stomping on them with their hooves, and they like to raid bird nests and snack on their eggs.

Your "funny bone" is not a bone - it's a nerve. When you bump your elbow, your ulnar nerve gets trapped between your skin and your humerus, the bone of your upper arm, and your reaction to the pain is often perceived as humorous.

Tigers are nicer than lions. They share their food, and males let the females and cubs eat first, but lions will fight
to the death over a kill.

Hundreds of people die shoveling snow each year. Those over 55 are advised not to shovel snow, because heart rate and blood pressure rise while cold air constricts arteries and limits blood supply. However, if you're young and healthy, shoveling snow can burn
600 calories an hour.

It's legal for a doctor to perform assisted suicide (giving a patient the knowledge and means to take their own life) in 5 different countries and 5 U.S. states. However, doctors are only allowed to cause a patient's death (euthanasia) in the Netherlands, Belgium, and Luxembourg.

Introverts and extroverts have differences in their brains. Studies show that introverts are easily over-stimulated and have thicker gray matter in the part of the brain linked to decision-making, while extroverts need more stimulation and have a greater response to risk and reward.

Perfectionism can be a curse that often leads to depression. According to psychologists, perfectionists may have unrealistic views about failure and are overly critical of themselves, which has a very negative impact on daily life.

Candy canes used to be straight, white sticks. Red stripes were added in the early 1900s, and now about 1.76 billion are sold annually during the holiday season alone.

The Coke logo has an unintentional hidden message. A Danish ad agency noticed Denmark's flag could be seen in the soda's logo, so they joined together to give out Danish Coca-Cola flags at the Copenhagen airport.

Sitting too close to the TV doesn't hurt your eyes. Kids who sit too close to the television won't damage their eyesight, but if they're doing it all the time they might already be nearsighted – not the other way around.

Reindeer make excellent "getaway cars."
In Siberia, people often use reindeer to
escape from crime scenes. The Russian
police are now asking to have their
snowmobiles replaced with reindeer.

William Shakespeare invented the word
swagger. In fact, he invented over 1,700
common words that we use today,
including: bedazzled, aroused, drugged,
addiction, puking, bloodstained, accused,
dauntless, assassination, cold-blooded,
elbow, and eyeball.

A little girl saved her dad's life after she learned fire safety from Sparkles the dog at a school seminar. When her house caught fire, she remembered what he taught her and crawled out to call for help. Her father, who would have burned to death, was saved just in time.

The American Civil War began and ended in the 2 homes of grocer Wilmer McLean. In 1861, Confederates used his house as a headquarters. Even though McLean moved 120 miles south to get away, Robert E. Lee surrendered to Ulysses S. Grant in the front parlor of McLean's new home.

Bullied or abused children age faster. A study found that children who suffer multiple incidents of violence experience faster biological aging and are more likely to die prematurely.

Increments of time can help put large numbers in perspective. While a million seconds equals 11.5 days, a billion seconds equals 32 years. And a trillion seconds? That's 32,000 years.

You can tour the Smithsonian without leaving your house. Washington D.C.'s National Museum of Natural History has a virtual tour of the entire museum that you can navigate with your desktop or mobile phone.

Soy sauce can kill you. A 19-year-old college student pledging a fraternity was dared to chug a quart of soy sauce and nearly died of hypernatremia, aka sodium poisoning. He was in a coma for 3 days but eventually made a full recovery.

Mexican free-tailed bats sabotage each other to steal food. They deliberately jam other bats' echolocation sonar when hunting insects, then swoop in and take the loot.

So many astronauts are from Ohio that NASA has a webpage dedicated to them. So far there have been 29, including John Glenn (1st in the USA to orbit Earth), Neil Armstrong (1st to step on the moon), and Jim Lovell (Apollo 11). Note: The Wright Bros (1st to fly) were also from Ohio.

Robin Williams' death helped save lives. The National Suicide Prevention Lifeline reported that it received the most calls in its history the day after Williams' death. The organization credited the bump in calls to the fact that many news stories included the hotline's number.

You can call a random Swedish person and talk to them about their country. The Swedish Tourist Association wants to encourage friendships between people in different countries, and they suggest conversation topics such as meatballs, darkness, suicide rates, politics, and the northern lights.

Making out is good for your body. An intense make-out session can double your metabolic rate, and it can also burn up to 2 calories per minute.

The oldest known Christmas menu, published in 'The Accomplisht Cook' in 1660, included steak pie, eels, lampreys, a swan roast, six woodcocks, powdered geese, jellies, and "a kid with a pudding in his belly."

Concrete Cowboys is a Philadelphia program that teaches inner-city kids responsibility and maturity through caring for and riding horses. The kids can also offer $5 rides in a nearby park, pocket half the proceeds, and use the other half to buy the horses' hay.

Spending money on others makes you happier than spending it on yourself. A recent study found that giving money to other people improves social connections, and people need other people (not possessions) to achieve true happiness.

Cats have whiskers so they can sense danger. When their whiskers brush against an object, cats can tell the exact location, size, and texture of it - even in the dark. They also use whiskers to determine whether they can fit in a tight space and to detect approaching dangers.

Your pupils dilate when you're looking at someone you love.

Approximately 20 American veterans commit suicide every day. On average, two of them are younger than 30.

Studies continue to suggest that antibacterial soaps have horrible side effects and very few benefits. The soaps can actually increase the risk of infection, make bacteria resistant to antibiotics, and contain harsh chemicals we're washing down the drain and into the ecosystem.

There are underground salt mines that people visit to ease their asthma. Each year thousands of patients spend weeks underground to treat their respiratory diseases. Some claim the mines have a unique micro-climate that reduces symptoms for years at a time.

Rattlesnakes like to eat squirrels, so the squirrels learned how to use snakeskin to their advantage. To avoid becoming snake-food, squirrels figured out they can mask their scent by chewing on shed snakeskin and then licking their own fur.

If you like singing Frank Sinatra songs, avoid karaoke in the Philippines. There have been at least half a dozen people killed for singing "My Way" at karaoke bars and probably many more injured. A lot of bars have removed the song from their books, and local news media has a crime category called "My Way Killings."

During WWII, the U.S. military considered sending kamikaze bats to the Japanese. They wanted to see if bats fitted with bombs could set fires around Japan, but the bats kept burning down the testing facilities.

Grumpy Cat is a millionaire. It's estimated that she has earned millions since the fall of 2012 due to her licensed merchandise, books, Friskies endorsement, 16 million YouTube views, and the Lifetime movie "Grumpy Cat's Worst Christmas Ever."

Women ranked men from Spain, Brazil, and Italy as the top 3 world's best lovers, according to a survey by OnePoll.com. The worst lovers? Men from Germany (too stinky), England (too lazy), and America (too rough).

If you're in bed a lot, you might be lonely. Studies suggest that lonely people spend more time in their beds, even though they have trouble sleeping. Chronic loneliness can cause insomnia, as well as the need to get in bed without feeling tired.

A 'blue moon' happens when there is an extra full moon during part of the year, but it isn't usually blue in color. It is a rare occurrence that only happens every few years, or, "once in a blue moon."

The telegraph was invented because of heartbreak. When Samuel Morse left town to paint a portrait, his wife suddenly fell ill and died. Because it took days for him to find out she had been sick, he was so upset that he abandoned his art career and focused on developing a fast method for long-distance communication.

In Manchester, two gay men singing songs from Wicked were attacked by a mob of 15 homophobic men after exiting the tram. Weeks later, 80 LGBT choir members boarded the tram and sang show tunes, gaining praise from the city council, tram operators, and police commissioner.

Most Americans will pay more for organic food, even though they don't know what it is. A 2014 study showed that 70% of shoppers were buying some sort of organic food, but 20% of them couldn't explain what "organic" food means.

Little people were well-respected in Ancient Egypt, and some were considered to be gods. The Egyptians were tolerant of many medical disorders, and they thought that caring for all people was a moral duty.

There's a legendary "monster" in Iceland called the Yule Cat that eats anyone who doesn't get new clothes for Christmas. Farmers used to warn their workers that the Yule Cat would come if they didn't process the autumn wool. If they obeyed, they'd receive new clothes. If not, they'd be eaten by the Yule Cat.

At any given moment, there are over 1,200 satellites orbiting the Earth, taking pictures and spying on you.

Feeling rejected is not much different from actual pain. Studies of MRI scans have shown that the same areas of the brain that respond to physical pain also react to being hurt by rejection. As far as your brain is concerned, a broken heart is no different than a broken arm.

A woman stopped eating to save people during WWII. Everyone was worried about nutrition because of food rations, so scientist Elsie Widdowson ate small amounts of bread, cabbage, and potatoes for months. She climbed mountains every day to prove that very little food was still enough. Her experiment formed the basic wartime diet of Britain.

30 million Americans recently reported suffering from an eating disorder at some point in their lives, and 1/3 of them were men.

You're completely blind for about 40 minutes a day. When your eyes move, your brain purposely blocks your vision, which is why you can't see the motion of your own eyes in a mirror. It's called Saccadic masking, and without it your life would be like watching a constant movie that's filmed with a shaky, handheld camera.

Beijing's pollution is so bad that people often stay indoors, and children have to play sports inside of inflatable, clean air domes.

If you're talking about the North Pole, you'll need to be more specific, because there are actually 7 of them: geographic north pole (true north), magnetic north pole, geomagnetic north pole, instantaneous north pole, celestial north pole, north pole of inaccessibility, and, lastly, the town of North Pole, Alaska.

During WWI, the British and German soldiers stopped fighting on Christmas. About 100,000 troops had a 'Christmas truce' in 1914 and crossed trenches to chat, exchange food and gifts, swap prisoners, play football, and sing carols together.

Fake smiles are more asymmetrical than real ones. Studies of facial expressions have shown that sincere smiles are often more symmetrical than those that are forced, which is why they look more pleasant.

Every hour you spend watching television shortens your lifespan by 22 minutes. Researchers say watching too much TV is just as bad as smoking, and that someone who watches 6 hours of TV a day risks losing 5 years of their life.

The world will end in about a billion years. All of Earth's water will eventually evaporate as the Sun becomes more luminous, and the planet is not expected to survive the Sun transitioning into a red giant.

A strong immune system won't keep you from catching a cold. Your body attacking the virus causes inflammation in your nose and throat, but the virus itself is harmless. Buying immune boosting products is like turning up the heater when you're already hot.

Following your heart could literally be the key to happiness. People who are the most aware of their own heartbeat have better intuition and are better at feeling, expressing, and recognizing emotions. Those who are less aware of their bodies feel more disconnected and have a higher rate of depression.

The Guinness World Records listing for the 'most prolific mother ever' is credited to an unnamed Russian peasant from the 1700s. She is rumored to have had 69 children and 27 pregnancies, resulting in '16 pairs of twins, 7 sets of triplets, and 4 sets of quadruplets.'

The universe has its own color. Scientists determined that the light from over 200,000 galaxies adds up to a beigeish-white. They call it "cosmic latte."

Every year, a wealthy Kansas City businessman known only as "Secret Santa" gives out $100,000 to random strangers. One year he asked local police officers to do it. They turned on their sirens and pulled people over, then surprised them with money, bringing many of them to tears.

Studies show that in a heterosexual relationship, when the woman frequently texts her partner they are both happier with each other. But as men text more, both partners feel less happy, and women often consider ending the relationship.

Men prefer bigger breasts for scientific reasons. A series of studies found that men who make less money, want to have kids someday, and are hungry (at the time of the study) prefer larger breasts, while men who are financially secure, don't want kids, and are full from a recent meal are more likely to enjoy small breasts.

Shocking your brain will make you better at math. Scientists have proven that a mild electric current, barely enough to light a light bulb, passing through the brain can improve a person's math abilities for 6 months.

U.S. army dogs are assigned higher ranks than their handlers. When the handler gets promoted, the dog is promoted as well.

General Mills markets Cinnamon Toast Crunch as a family brand, because adults account for nearly half of its consumption, and it's known to be a popular snack for gamers.

There's a much faster way to board a plane that airlines aren't using. Not charging passengers to check bags and seating every 2 rows at a time (instead of every seat in order from front to back) could reduce boarding time by 30%.

Your future password could be your pulse. The Nymi is a wristband that you can tap against a terminal to verify your identity with your pulse pattern. Fingerprints and PIN numbers can be easily copied or stolen, but your heartbeat is unique to you and can't be replicated.

Freerice.com is a charity website that quizzes you and donates 10 grains of rice to the World Food Programme each time you get a correct answer. Every question pertains to word definitions, so you get to play a game, keep your mind sharp, and help feed the hungry all at the same time.

Neuroscientists prescribe video games for people with autism and Asperger's so they can practice social interaction in a safe, non-threatening environment. This eases anxiety and allows users to gain confidence and apply it in their daily lives.

Many people dropped out of the 2014 Beijing marathon because their mask filters turned gray after a few miles. Researchers describe the atmosphere as nearly "uninhabitable for human beings."

Music can make your heart dance. Studies show that the body's breathing and heart rate changes rhythm and synchronizes to the music that's being played, which can explain why you get chills when listening to something awesome.

Charity Miles is an app that helps you earn money for your charity every time you walk, bike, or run. You pick the charity, the app tracks your distance, and up to 25 cents per mile is donated on your behalf.

In the Victorian era, there were special moustache cups for drinking tea. The cup kept men's moustache wax out of the tea so it wouldn't melt into their cup when they took a sip.

10-year-old Tom Phillips saved his dad's life. They were working on the farm when a bull suddenly attacked and charged his father. Tom didn't know how to drive and was forbidden to use the tractor, but he jumped in and pushed the bull away. His Mom thinks he's a hero, but he didn't want her to know he drove the tractor because he felt guilty about breaking the rules.

Strippers make more money in tips when they are ovulating. A study followed strippers for 2 months and showed that they earn about $75 to $150 more per shift during ovulation.

The center of the Milky Way tastes like raspberries and smells like Captain Morgan. Astronomers researching the giant dust cloud in the middle of the galaxy found the chemical ethyl formate, which gives raspberries their flavor and smells like rum.

Thomas Edison took a video of Mark Twain in 1909. The silent film shows Twain walking around his Connecticut property in his signature white suit, smoking a cigar, and having tea with his daughters. It is the only existing footage of him and was taken a year before he died.

If you could dig a hole through the Earth and jump in (without dying), you would not come out the other side. You'd fall down for 20 minutes until you reached the center, then technically you'd be considered 'falling up' until you made it to the opposite surface - where you'd fall down, over and over again.
Forever.

Coffee beans are not beans. They are actually seeds, which are often called "coffee cherries."

The next generation of elevators will be able to travel sideways. A German engineering company has created the world's 1st rope-free elevator system, which uses a new magnetic technology. The design will create a smaller footprint and allow building designs to be greener.

Blowing your nose too hard makes you more congested. When you're "stuffed up," its because of swollen blood vessels, not excess snot. Hard blowing shoves mucus up into your sinuses and slows the drainage process. You should either blow softly, or snort and swallow.

Internet porn can be as addictive as taking drugs. Just like a user chasing his first high, watching too much online porn numbs the effect of dopamine in your brain until you can no longer be aroused, and quitting causes withdrawal symptoms.

Harper Lee wrote her famous novel because she was given the best Christmas present ever. In 1956, friends gave her a note that said "You have one year off to write whatever you please. Merry Christmas." They supported her with a year's wages, and she wrote "To Kill a Mockingbird."

Women only spend about 39 seconds longer in the shower than men, but people between 18 and 24 take showers that are at least 5 minutes longer than people over 55, according to research.

In the 1800s, a man was convicted of murdering his wife because her ghost "visited" her mother and accused him. The ghost's "testimony" was used in court to show the jury that the mother was crazy, but she was so convincing they found him guilty - even though there was no evidence.

Elephants are fighting poachers with evolution. An increasing number of elephants are being born tuskless. Experts think this could be due to males with the biggest tusks being hunted, so the smaller tusked males are doing more breeding.

When you die, there are companies that will turn your ashes into fireworks so you can literally "go out with a bang."

124

Kathrine Switzer competed in the Boston Marathon before women were allowed to enter. In 1967, a race official tried to physically remove her from the race, but her boyfriend pushed him down. She was the 1st woman to ever finish the race as a numbered entry.

9-year-old Anaiah Tucker jumped in front of a speeding truck to push her sister out of the way. She broke her neck and lost a leg, but says it was worth it to save her 5-year-old sister, who she thought was "too young to be hit" and would have been "gone forever."

Mental illnesses cause more years lived with disability than any other disease worldwide. The greatest amount of years people live with a disability are due to neuropsychiatric disorders, and the majority of those are anxiety and major depressive disorder.

Larry Flynt, founder of Hustler magazine, doesn't want the white supremacist who shot and paralyzed him to get the death penalty because "a life spent in a 3-by-6-foot cell is far harsher than the quick release of a lethal injection."

In 1983, Michael Jackson's "Thriller" video played for a week at a movie theater so it could qualify for an Oscar nomination, but it opened for Disney's Fantasia and terrified the children. It did not get nominated.

Every December 25th, a town in Peru celebrates 'Takanakuy.' Men, women, and children settle grudges from the past year by calling each other out and having a fist fight. Then everybody goes drinking to numb the pain and move on to a new year.

Falling in love is similar to the feeling of using cocaine. Both experiences activate the same brain chemicals and structures, causing a better mood, increase in sexual appetite, higher self-esteem, and greater consciousness.

There are hermaphrodite sea slugs with disposable penises. While all sea slugs have both male and female parts, the Chromodoris reticulata is the only species that can have sex, detach its penis, and then grow a new one within 24 hours.

Stem cells could extend the lives of future humans. Scientists injected mice that normally live 21 days with stem cells and they lived about 70 days, which is like an 80-year-old human living to be 200.

You can argue all day about whether it's more painful to go through childbirth or to be kicked in the balls, but no one will ever agree because pain is relative. Since people have different tolerance levels and coping skills, "what hurts more" will never be determined.

Sergeant Stubby, the 'Hero Dog of WWI,' once caught a German soldier by the seat of his pants and held him until American soldiers came. He also served in 17 battles, saved his regiment from surprise mustard gas attacks, and helped locate wounded soldiers.

There are speed bumps that reward you for slowing down. Designers created a speed bump that flattens for those who drive over it slowly, but people who go too fast will still get a jolt.

Merkins are pubic wigs worn by actresses who don't have enough pubes or need to cover their genitalia during nude scenes in a film. Women used them in the 1400s when they shaved themselves to combat pubic lice, and prostitutes wore them to hide their syphilis. Note: sometimes they are made of beaver fur.

Heart surgery evolved thanks to Werner Forssman. In 1929, he believed you could insert a catheter into the heart. People said he was crazy, so he put a catheter into his own heart to prove it. Even though it worked, he got fired. Then he became a Nazi, but still won the Nobel Prize... and then he died of heart failure.

On the Norwegian Island of Spitsbergen, sitting 427 feet inside a mountain, is the Svalbard Global Seed Vault, which holds over 850,000 seeds from around the planet in case of global catastrophe.

Sunlight is good for your body and mind. Spending time in the sun can improve your health, make you happier, help you relax, boost your concentration, decrease your pain, and help you heal faster.

Lay your arm on a flat surface and push your thumb and pinky together. If you don't see a raised band extending down from your wrist, you are a product of evolution. If you do, you've got a useless extra muscle in your arm that is slowly being erased from our genetic code.

Being gay used to be classified as a medical disorder in Sweden, so on August 29, 1979, a bunch of folks called in gay to work - including a woman who was able to collect welfare benefits. Homosexuality was declassified as a disease within 2 months.

Stephen Hawking threw a party for time-travelers on June 28, 2009. His invitations were sent out the next day, but nobody showed up. This, he claims, is experimental evidence that proves time travel is not possible.

Holding your key fob up to your chin when trying to lock your door from afar will increase its range by several car lengths. Your head is filled with fluid, so it acts as a conductor that sends the signal even further than its natural reach.

Babies may practice crying in the womb. Researchers have videos of 3rd-trimester fetuses that appear to be silently crying in response to being startled by noises played on the mother's abdomen.

Ashley Revell sold everything he owned, went to Vegas, bet all his money on red at a roulette table, and won $236,000. He hadn't known which color he would pick, but when the wheel started to spin, "red" popped into his head. He spent some of his winnings traveling to Europe, where he ended up meeting his future wife.

If you have a hot temper, you could be suffering from cat rage. Scientists discovered toxoplasmosis, an infection spread by cats that's linked to various mental disorders, may have the potential to induce enraging mood swings. One study showed some infected people were twice as likely to experience unreasonable outbursts of anger.

Knowing more than one language keeps your brain young and forces it to be more flexible. Studies show degenerative disorders like Alzheimer's and dementia are delayed by up to 5 years in bilingual people.

There are over 645 different meanings of the word 'run.'

Early American humans used to hunt giant armadillos and live inside their shells. Glyptodons were large, armored mammals that grew to the size of a Volkswagen Beetle, and natives took shelter inside their gigantic shells.

Dropbox CEO Drew Houston's advice to his younger self would be a tennis ball and the number 30,000. When he was 24 he realized the average person lives 30,000 days, and 8,000 of his days were already gone. The tennis ball is a reminder to go after what you want the way a dog chases a ball, because you've only got 30,000 days to catch it.

Population.io tells you when you will die. After entering your birthday, the site shows you your life expectancy, the number of people who share your birthday, and how many people in the world are younger than you. Note: You're older than you think.

Your beard is making you healthier. Growing a beard has actual health benefits, such as preventing allergies, asthma attacks, and rashes, and protecting your skin from the sun.

Dolphins can make their own toys. When a dolphin snorts underwater, they produce bubble rings (toroidal vortices) that they play with by swimming through them, tossing them around, and biting them.

Tetris has been used to treat adults that have a lazy eye. Researchers studied the effects of using a video game to force both eyes to work together, and they found that the patients treated with Tetris showed a four-fold improvement in their lazy eye compared to those who were patched.

If you like smelling your dog's feet, you're not alone. Most dogs have bacteria on their paws that make them smell like corn chips, which is commonly referred to as "Frito feet."

Mammals with bigger balls are more likely to kill babies. Because of what's called "sperm competition," animals that have the largest testicles have a greater desire to father as many offspring as possible and are more likely to kill the children of their rivals.

Studies show 86% of vegetarians and 70% of vegans eventually start eating meat again, especially later in life. Researchers suggest that this is mostly due to an all-veggie diet being very difficult for most people to accomplish.

The more you trust people, the better you are at spotting liars. A recent study showed that people who put faith in the honesty of others were more accurate when determining if someone was lying to them.

Helen Keller was good friends with Charlie Chaplin. They were both shunned for their social and political views, and she was considered a radical because she supported women and the disabled. It wasn't until the end of her life that she was finally recognized with honor.

Tobacco could be used to fuel airplanes in the future. A new type of tobacco plant grown in South Africa produces oil that converts into biofuel and could lower carbon emissions by 80%.

The Orion spacecraft took special artifacts on its 2014 test flight. As it flew 15 times higher than the International Space Station, it brought along a T Rex fossil, a piece of an Apollo 11 spacesuit, and two Sesame Street mementos: Cookie Monster's cookie and Ernie's rubber ducky.

Flu shots are more important than you think. The CDC recommends that all children from 6 mos to 18 yrs should have an annual shot, but only about half do. Influenza killed 149 children between 2012 and 2013. 90% of them weren't vaccinated. Flu shots increase a child's chance of not even needing to see a doctor by 60%.

The human body is thought to have 7 octillion atoms, also known as a seven followed by 27 zeros, or 7,000,000,000,000,000,000,000,000,000.

Madagascar is home to leaf-tailed geckos, whose bodies look exactly like dead leaves, moss, or tree bark. They come in many shades to match different structures in their habitats, and some even hang from branches like real leaves when they feel threatened.

Action gamers are better learners. They excel at predicting the sequence of upcoming events and become better learners by playing fast-paced games, according to a recent study.

The idea of scorpion suckers came from people's obsession with tequila shots. In the 1980s, the founder of Hotlix Candy made a tequila-flavored lollipop with a real worm in the middle, which escalated into a variety of crunchy, insect-filled candies.

Thanksgiving is an official holiday due to the author of "Mary Had a Little Lamb." Sarah Josepha Hale wrote to 5 different U.S. presidents asking them to make Thanksgiving a national holiday, finally convincing Abraham Lincoln in 1863.

"Twinkle, Twinkle, Little Star," the "Alphabet Song," and "Baa, Baa, Black Sheep" all have the same melody that evolved from a naughty French rhyme about a girl who tells her mother she was seduced. The rhyme was later added to a melody that's still being used for many songs in different cultures.

As humans evolved, skulls grew and jaws
shrunk to make room for larger brains.
Since our teeth stayed the same size,
'wisdom' teeth don't fit anymore. If you
were born without them, you're
one of the lucky 35%.

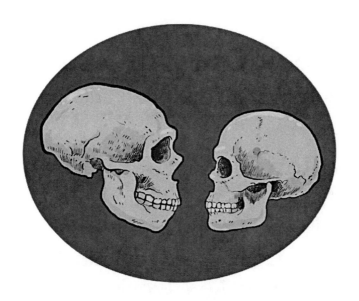

In 1998, schools bought pencils that said
"TOO COOL TO DO DRUGS" on them.
A 4th grader finally realized that
sharpening them removed the "too,"
making it "cool to do drugs" and then
simply saying "do drugs" as they were
used up. They were recalled, but now
you can buy them for fun.

Get more amazing facts every single day from Did You Know!

Check Out Our Articles

http://DidYouKnowFacts.com

Follow Us For Daily Facts

Facebook: @didyouknowblog
Twitter: @didyouknowfacts
Instagram: @didyouknowblog
YouTube: @didyouknowblog

Get Facts Texted To You

http://Fact-Snacks.com

CPSIA information can be obtained
at www.ICGtesting.com
Printed in the USA
FFOW03n1306221216
30695FF

9 780998 205007